Sport

Jim Kerr

W
FRANKLIN WATTS
LONDON • SYDNEY

First published in 2009 by
Franklin Watts
338 Euston Road
London NW1 3BH

Franklin Watts Australia
Level 17/207 Kent Street
Sydney NSW 2000

Series editor: Julia Bird
Design: Nimbus Design

A CIP catalogue record for this book is available
from the British Library.

ISBN 978 0 7496 8865 3

Dewey classification: 306.48'3

Picture credits:
Mario Anzuoni/Reuters/Corbis: 36. AP/PA Photos: 29.
Matthew Ashton/AMA/Corbis: 15. Diego Azbuel/epa/Corbis: 38.
Laurent Baheux/TempSport/Corbis: front cover. Matt Baron/Rex Features: 9.
David Bergman/Corbis: 21. Bettmann/Corbis: 11. Derek Cattani/Rex Features: 34. Corbis: 30.
Carlos Dominguez/Corbis: 17. DPA/PA Photos: 16. Peter Foley/epa/Corbis: 31.
Victor Fraile/Corbis: 25. Golf Picture Bank/Alamy: 32. Robert Hallam/Rex Features: 33.
Ho/Reuters/Corbis: 27. Steve Lipofsky/Corbis: 18. Leo Mason/Corbis: 23.
Frank May/epa/Corbis: 41r. LucyNicholson/Reuters/Corbis: 13. Offside/Rex Features: 24.
PA Archive/PA Photos: 8. Doug Peters/Pa Photos: 41l. Reuters/Corbis: 26.
Rex Features: 19, 37. Chris Ryan/Corbis: 28. Tim de Waele/Corbis: 39.
Tim Wimbourne/Reuters/Corbis: 20.

Printed in Malaysia

Franklin Watts is a division of Hachette Children's Books,
an Hachette UK company.
www.hachette.co.uk

Contents

King of the track

In November 2008, Lewis Hamilton became the youngest ever Formula One World Champion. The 24-year-old's achievement was front page news across the world. In the week that he became world champion, Lewis received as much coverage in the media as the most famous politicians, actors and pop stars.

Hamilton's career tells us a lot about the power of the media in sport. Huge coverage ensures that top Formula One drivers can earn millions of pounds in endorsements and become famous public figures. By the age of 13, Hamilton had been signed by McLaren racing team to their Young Driver Support Programme. As the young driver rose through the ranks, his career was closely followed in the media. In order to succeed, Hamilton needed to have a cool head at the wheel. He also needed to be able to deal with the pressure that comes with the glare of publicity.

Role model

Hamilton has what it takes to succeed at the highest level. He is a winner, who takes a single-minded approach to achieve success. He is also the first non-white racing driver to become Formula One World Champion. His success

Lewis Hamilton meets the media as the new Formula One World Champion.

shows that all athletes, regardless of race or religion, can compete at the highest level. When it comes to his ability to negotiate sponsorship, Hamilton is in pole position. Already the face of a famous bank, Lewis Hamilton is likely to saturate the media in the coming years.

In the spotlight

But this success comes at a price. Hamilton is now expected to act in a way that is appropriate for a role model. Public interest is no longer confined to Lewis Hamilton the racing driver. The media want to know about every aspect of his life away from the track. Any scandal would be all over the front pages. Lewis Hamilton has already indicated that the power of the media can be too much. In 2007, he moved to Switzerland to escape the non-stop media attention he faced in the UK.

Lewis Hamilton has added to his media fame by teaming up with the lead singer of a girl band, Nicole Scherzinger of The Pussycat Dolls. Their relationship has been widely reported in the press.

• *Up for discussion* •

Do you think it is fair that sportspeople like Lewis Hamilton are expected to be role models for young people? What do we expect from role models?

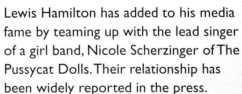

Using the media

At great sporting events, such as the Olympics, the technological power of the media is plain to see. But the media's power in sport can be seen in other ways, too.

Lighting the way

Countries have often used sporting events to demonstrate their views or achievements to the rest of the world. The Olympic Games are an international celebration of the excellence of the human race. However, there can be intense rivalry between individual countries.

The Olympic spirit requires the Games to take place in an arena free of politics. This was challenged during the 1980s, when the USSR (now Russia) and its Eastern neighbours were involved in a period of political tension with the USA and its Western supporters, known as the Cold War. Following the 1979 USSR invasion of Afghanistan, the USA pulled out of the 1980 games in Moscow, Russia. Four years later, the USSR boycotted the Los Angeles Olympic Games.

Case study: The 1936 Berlin Olympics

Germany in the 1930s was ruled by the National Socialist, or Nazi, party. The party and its leader, Adolf Hitler, held extreme views. They were hostile to Jews, and believed in the supremacy of a 'master' Aryan race made up of people of north European descent.

The 1936 Olympic Games were held in the capital of Germany, Berlin. Nazi leaders saw this as an opportunity to use the media attention attracted by the Games to put out information supporting their ideas – a powerful political tool known as propaganda.

The German Olympic team was dominated by members of the so-called Aryan race. Although Germany won most of the medals during the Games, African-American athlete Jesse Owens (opposite) won four gold medals, breaking world records in three events.

The Nazis celebrated the success of Aryan athletes in newspaper reports and in the film Olympia. But the world's media celebrated the triumphs of other athletes, in particular Jesse Owens. Owens' achievements had discredited 'white supremacy' beliefs.

The flame goes out

The Olympic boycotts of the 1980s played on the huge power of media in sport. Driven in part by a refusal to participate in celebrating the achievements of the host nation, the boycotts reminded the world's media of the ongoing hostility between the Cold War nations.

The most horrific hijacking of the Olympic spirit occurred in Munich in 1972. Members of a Palestinian terrorist group seized the world's attention when they kidnapped and killed eleven Israeli athletes directly in the view of the world's media.

• *Up for discussion* •

The Olympic spirit attempts to build a peaceful and better world through a spirit of friendship, solidarity and fair play.
How can the media support these goals?

Jesse Owens' record-breaking success in the 1936 Olympic Games made him a household name across the world.

Global games

Nowhere is the power of the media demonstrated more clearly than in the USA. Although sports such as baseball and American football are hardly played outside the USA, global media coverage ensures that these sports have a huge international following.

Only in America

American football grew out of football and rugby and is played only in the USA and Canada. Baseball was a development of cricket and is North America's summer game. However, with the exception of Japan, there are no major professional leagues in other countries. Basketball was invented by an American sports teacher in 1891. There are leagues in some European countries, but the strongest league is the US NBA (National Basketball Association). Ice hockey is hardly played outside North America.

• Up for discussion •

Fees for an advertising slot during the Superbowl are US $3 million for a 30-second commercial. Why do you think advertisers are willing to pay so much?

Case study: The Superbowl — a global event

US sport and entertainment combine at the most powerful level in the Superbowl and its accompanying 'Half-Time Show'. The Superbowl is watched by close to 100 million people. But for many viewers, the highlight of the event is the Half-Time Show, featuring television and popular music stars. The show costs millions of dollars to stage, and employs hundreds of people. It is a powerful media event, and one that celebrates the way of life in the USA.

The show

US sports often cross into the entertainment industry. The Harlem Globetrotters are one of the most famous basketball teams in the world. But they do not play real games. Instead they play 'exhibition' matches, entertaining the crowd with trick shots and comedy plays. They have also appeared on television.

Global hoops

Such is the power of the US sports media that basketball is now the leading national sport in China. In 1987, China's national television station, China Central Television (CCTV), was offered an incredible deal for television rights to NBA games. The NBA agreed to share money from advertisers with the Chinese television company. But in the early years of coverage, there was little interest in basketball among Chinese viewers and no advertising for the games. The NBA sent the money from advertisers anyway, so it was effectively paying to televise US games in China.

NBA China

The NBA has fed and encouraged interest in basketball in China in the two decades since 1987. 14 NBA games are now broadcast live every week on state television. In 2008, NBA China was set up with support from US entertainment and media giant Disney. The explosion of basketball in China, the world's most populated country, means that it has overtaken football as the world's leading participation sport. The international football body, FIFA, estimates that 270 million people play football worldwide. It is thought that more than 300 million people now play basketball.

The most famous Chinese basketball player of all time, Yao Ming, plays in the NBA for the Houston Rockets. His first season with the Rockets was captured in a documentary called *The Year of the Yao*.

Big business

Why are sports stars paid such huge sums of money? At the top level, professional athletes and teams, no matter which sport they play, are highly valuable. However, the media appearances of the top teams and players are often just as important as their performance on the field.

Media players

Media exposure helps to generate the publicity that keeps a team or player in the public eye. Successful sports teams with global popularity can earn millions of pounds from television companies in return for the right to broadcast their games. They can also sign 'mega-buck' sponsorship deals with businesses. The top sports teams are huge, multi-million pound organisations, often powerful media businesses in their own right.

Big business

The most successful sports teams receive huge media attention, and have become powerful media players. The combination of success on the field, together with enormous media power, has proved irresistible to other businesses.

Many of the top sports teams are now owned by some of the world's wealthiest people. The Dallas Cowboys American football team is owned by Jerry Jones, who struck it rich in natural gas in the 1970s. Silvio Berlusconi, Italy's prime minister and richest person, built a personal fortune through media interests. He became president of AC Milan FC (football club) in 1986. US businessman Malcolm Glazer has put together a global sports empire – he bought the Tampa Bay Buccaneers American football team in 1995, and ten years later, took over UK football team Manchester United (see p.15).

• Up for discussion •

The enormous power that tycoon-backed football teams now hold is being questioned. FIFA President Sepp Blatter has said, 'It seems these days you can buy a club as easily as you buy a football jersey.' What do you think could be the drawbacks of this?

Case study: Red Devils

Manchester United Football Club (MUFC) has seized the opportunity to market its famous history and success on the field in the 21st century. It was one of the first clubs to position itself as not simply a football team, but a business. It was also one of the first football clubs to become a company listed on the stock market. MUFC is currently the richest club in football, with a value of nearly £900 million as of May 2008.

How has it managed to do this? Manchester United has as many as 75 million fans worldwide, and 80 per cent of the fan base is outside the UK. MUFC has needed to communicate with these fans, particularly in the USA and Asia.

In order to do this, Manchester United has developed a media empire using the latest global technology. This includes a dedicated television channel, MUTV, the ManUtd.com website, MU.TV online, a Chinese language website and MU mobile phones. The club even has its own cinema and recently opened its first café in China, named 'One United'. Here, Asian fans can purchase yearbooks, magazines and other media merchandise.

With over 40 million fans in Asia, the marketing team at MUFC has carefully built up a relationship with the team's supporters, turning them into lifelong customers of the club's products.

'Show me the money'

Some of the most powerful players in the sports and media mix are sports agents and marketing companies. These are the people who put together sponsorship deals. The world's biggest sporting events have television audiences of hundreds of millions. This is also a huge audience for a sponsor's advertising slogans and logos.

Pitching the product

Sport and advertising have an important relationship. Advertisers rely on the exposure that their products and services receive at sports events, and the attraction of sports stars as healthy, successful role models is used as 'pulling power' by many companies. In sport, income from advertising makes some events possible. The cost of running a Formula One team, for example, is huge and could not be met without sponsorship.

Marlboro, the cigarette brand, is heavily involved in sponsoring motor racing. But many people argue that tobacco companies should not be involved in advertising in sport, with its emphasis on fitness and health. Tobacco advertising is already banned at many sports events, and there have been moves to ban tobacco advertising at all events in recent years.

Formula One drivers Kimi Raikkonen and Felipe Massa show off their sponsors' logos at the Bahrain Grand Prix.

Most major sporting events are awash with sponsors' logos and advertisement billboards. But Wimbledon, one of the biggest tennis tournaments in the world, features very little advertising. There are only two brand names on view: IBM and Rolex. The organisers believe that the game comes first, followed by the branding of the organisers (the All-England Lawn Tennis Club) and finally the sponsors. Competitors must wear traditional, all-white uniforms.

With just two small and discreet sponsors' names, it is possible that 'less is more'. By limiting branding, tournament organisers hope to ensure that the high-class nature of the Wimbledon brand remains intact. This allows them to trade on the classic reputation of Wimbledon around the world. Wimbledon merchandise is now marketed heavily in India, China and Japan.

On Wimbledon's green-striped tennis lawns there is plenty of room for advertising billboards, but Wimbledon prefers spectators to focus on the tennis.

• Up for discussion •

At many sports events, a percentage of seats are given over to sponsors and their employees. Many complain that this prevents real fans from attending. But without the sponsors' money, the event may not happen. Which is more important, keeping the fans happy or the sponsors?

Sports idols

At the very pinnacle of sport is a group of stars who are household names; their faces may be familiar even to those who have no interest in sport. Many use their media fame to do good works.

Some stars are so famous they are known to all by nicknames that bestow a level of greatness. Like royalty, they are above ordinary human beings. Basketball great Michael Jordan was often referred to as 'His Airness'. This nickname is a supreme example of the power of media in sport. It demonstrates that Jordan had reached the level of sporting royalty. But it also suggests that his trademarked footwear – Nike Air Jordan's – may have lifted him there.

Good sports

Many sports icons use their media profile for good causes. Footballer David Beckham, for example, (see p.19) has supported the children's charity UNICEF since his days at Manchester United. Boxing legend Muhammad Ali also carries out important work on behalf of UNICEF, and, in recognition of his work for the United Nations, was named in 2002 as a UN cultural ambassador, or 'messenger for peace'.

Michael Jordan is widely acclaimed as the greatest ever basketball player.

Star quality

Companies compete to secure the most celebrated sportsmen and women to endorse their products, which can range from trainers and tennis raquets to razors, underwear and fizzy drinks. These deals can potentially make millions both for the company and for the sports star.

Case study: **Brand it like Beckham**

Footballer David Beckham's fame extends way beyond the football pitch. In much of the world, his name may be 'as instantly recognisable as that of companies like Coca-Cola.'

Beckham's marriage to Victoria Beckham, the former Spice Girl, has always received huge media attention. Early on they were dubbed 'Posh and Becks' and their wedding was a worldwide media event, covered in an exclusive £1 million deal with OK! magazine.

The Beckhams have a team of people who carefully manage their public image and help to arrange lucrative advertising deals with global companies. The Beckhams have been paid by clothes designers, cosmetics manufacturers and producers of luxury goods to advertise their brands. They have used their fame to launch a joint fashion label – DVB – which sells everything from sunglasses to perfume.

Footballer David Beckham earns around £20 million a year from endorsements.

• *Up for discussion* •

Are there any products that are off-limits to sports star endorsement?

Would you prefer to buy a product advertised by a celebrity? Why?

Shooting stars

Sustained sporting excellence can earn great success and great wealth. But sporting stars, like shooting ones, can burn brightly before quickly fading away.

Cricket superstar

Even while still at school in Mumbai, Sachin Tendulkar was seen as destined for greatness. He set the cricketing world alight when he made his debut for the Indian team aged 16. For 20 years, the 'Little Master' has lived his sporting and personal life in the glare of the media spotlight in a country where cricket is a national obsession. But he has not blinked or stumbled. He is now the highest-run scorer in test cricket and one day internationals (ODIs).

Falling short

But for every Tendulkar there is a Freddy Adu. At 14, Adu became the youngest US athlete in over 100 years to sign a major league professional contract and was chosen by soccer team DC United as the number one pick in the 2004 Major League Soccer draft. But some commentators said that he was too young to play professionally. They argued that Adu needed time to develop, away from the media spotlight. Adu's star has since faded. The 20-year-old is currently struggling to make the first team at French side Monaco.

Sachin Tendulkar is a sporting and media icon in India. Almost any product he advertises is bound to be successful.

Teen golf sensation Michelle Wie has experienced more highs and lows than most senior pros. A top-ten finish in a major competition at the age of just 13 began the media hysteria. Newspapers hyped the young star with the first of the Tiger Woods comparisons.

Wie turned professional in October 2005, six days before her 16th birthday. The media interest intensified. First, multi-million-dollar sponsorship deals with Nike, Sony and Omega were secured. Then she switched to the men's events, having already become the youngest player to compete in a US men's tournament. In 2006, Wie was named by Time magazine as 'one of 100 people who shape our world'.

But things went horribly wrong for Wie in 2007. She injured both wrists, which affected her ability to hit the ball. She then returned to competition golf too soon. A succession of high-profile withdrawals and injuries at tournaments followed. Media stories claiming that Wie had achieved 'too much, too soon' began to appear. Although she is said to be rebuilding her game, Michelle Wie is a long way from becoming the golf powerhouse that the media predicted.

Michelle Wie is a professional golfer who has already banked more than US $30 million. But almost all of this money is from endorsements and not prize money from performances.

• Up for discussion •

Do you think media interest in young sportspeople is helpful or harmful to them? Why?

One newspaper said of Michelle Wie, 'Whatever way you look at it, the game needs characters and stars. These are the lifeblood of any professional sport'. Why do you think this is?

Crossing over

Many athletes have used their sporting celebrity to cross over into other entertainment sectors or sections of the media. Many ex-players put their insight into the game and continued access to the changing room to good use in newspaper columns. Others bring their inside knowledge of the game to television sports coverage.

Media angel

Gary Lineker was one of England's top football players, and is one of the best-known television sports presenters in the UK. He has developed a relaxed, jokey style with other former players-turned-pundits. His broadcaster, the BBC, also trades on Gary's 'nice-guy' image – he famously never received a booking during his entire playing career – to broaden his appeal.

• Up for discussion •

What can former players bring to media work?

What, apart from publicity, might tempt a sports star into appearing on TV?

Media devil

Unlike Gary Lineker, footballer Vinnie Jones gained a reputation and many red cards as a no-holds-barred defender while playing for Wimbledon FC in the 1990s. On retiring from football, Jones used the notoriety he had gained on the pitch to launch a film career playing villains, first in *Lock, Stock and Two Smoking Barrels* in 1998. He has now made over 30 appearances as a movie hard man.

Other former sports stars have used their fame to forge a media career in more varied ways. Olympic swimming legend Ian Thorpe (nicknamed the 'Thorpedo') is still seen at swimming competitions. However, to some, he appears more interested in the glitz and glam of the fashion and entertainment worlds – appearing in fashion shows and as an extra in the US sitcom *Friends*. He has even appeared in his own TV series *Undercover Angels,* but it was a spectacular flop.

Case study: Keeping her eye on the ball

Serena Williams is a good example of a sports star who has used her fame to cross over into the world of entertainment. She is interested in fashion and is well known for her striking on-court outfits, which have led to deals with Puma and Nike to design special lines of tennis wear.

Williams also courts attention away from the tennis arena. She has appeared in a number of advertisements and has also made a number of TV appearances. These include a reality show based on the lives of Serena and her sister Venus. She has also guest-starred in episodes of ER and Law & Order. And she has branched out into music, appearing in a video alongside Alicia Keys and hip hop artists Common and Kanye West.

In 2006, it looked as if this media work might be affecting Serena Williams' tennis. She dropped out of the Top 100 tennis rankings for the first time in a decade. But in 2008, the Williams sisters showed that they are true champions. They contested the Wimbledon Ladies final and later on the same day, won the Women's doubles final. Serena followed this by winning the women's title at the Australian Open in 2009. The Williams sisters keep sport first. By doing so, in spite of their media work, they have stayed at the top for a long time.

In her 14-year-career, Serena Williams has won every major title in tennis.

High pressure

The media is often guilty of creating hype around a sports star or competition. This can increase pressure on athletes; sometimes to the point where playing to win switches to winning at all costs.

Fair play

In the days before professionalism, amateur sports followed strict codes of conduct. These celebrated the values of fair play, accepting the decisions of officials, and taking defeat with good grace. But professional sport often elevates winning above sportsmanship.

Putting on the pressure

Liverpool FC manager Bill Shankly famously said: 'Some people believe football is a matter of life and death. It is much more important than that.' The media can often support the view that winning is everything in professional sports. This can put an intolerable amount of pressure on athletes.

Respect the referee

With its wall-to-wall television coverage, the stakes get no higher than in Premier League football. Professional fouls, gamesmanship and time-wasting are just some of the unsporting elements that spoil the spectacle of a top match for spectators. At its ugliest level, playing to win has led players into confrontations with referees. During the 2008 season, all clubs joined the 'Get On With The Game' media campaign, which put responsibility on club captains to control their team-mates and respect referees' decisions.

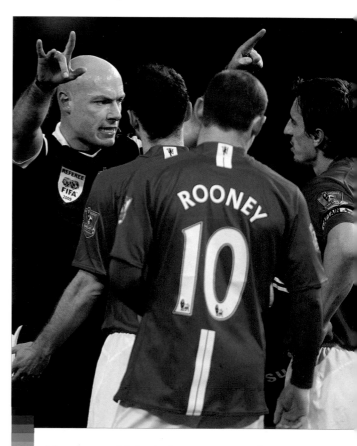

Manchester United players surround the referee during a tense Premier League match.

The media loves a champion who plays to win but is gracious in defeat; who does not question the umpire's decision; who behaves in an exemplary manner away from the field of play; and who is happy to undertake press conferences and media commitments. Roger Federer is a great example. The Swiss tennis champ is one of the greatest men's players ever. But he is also polite, immaculately dressed and perfectly behaved on court.

The opposite of Federer in his playing days was tennis player John McEnroe. An extremely talented player, McEnroe's on-court tantrums and outbursts and constant questioning of umpires' decisions made him unpopular among fans of the game and earned him the nickname 'SuperBrat' in the British press.

Since retiring from professional tennis, however, McEnroe has matured to become an informed and articulate, if occasionally outspoken, TV tennis commentator.

Roger Federer in action at the Australian Open in 2009.

• *Up for discussion* •

Does the media operate a double standard by on the one hand celebrating the achievements of sporting role models like Roger Federer, while at the same time focusing on the behaviour of 'bad boys' like John McEnroe?

Making headlines

On the biggest sporting stages, such as the Olympics or football World Cup finals, the media will often focus on one particular event or game. The media will work this story up to capture the public imagination.

Under the spotlight

Sometimes, the story involves intense rivalry between two stars or teams. The media might focus, for instance, on the contest between a king or queen of the track or ring and a young pretender to the crown. In some cases, the big story includes non-sporting elements, for example the background or personal life of an athlete.

Carrying a nation's hopes

In the 2000 Olympic Games, Cathy Freeman's participation in the women's 400 metres was the big story. Freeman was an Aboriginal athlete, competing for Australia in the host city of Sydney. She had overcome discrimination and crossed racial boundaries to get there.

The entire Australian nation was behind Cathy Freeman and the world's media could not get enough of her. Her anticipated victory was put across in the media as a reconciliation between white and Aboriginal Australians. There was never a sense that the women's 400 metres final was just another race.

Cathy Freeman proudly waves the Australian flag after winning the women's 400 metres final at the 2000 Olympic Games.

Case study: A moment of madness

The 2006 World Cup final between France and Italy was also the final game in the career of the legendary French midfield player, Zinedine Zidane. Zidane had scored with a penalty early in the game. But deep into extra time, with the score tied at 1-1, Zidane was sent off following a scuffle with Italian defender Marco Materazzi. He could not participate in the penalty shootout, which Italy won 5-3.

The incident received huge media coverage. Zidane was a legendary player and his actions seemed to have cost France the final. But there was more to the story. Zidane is famously of Algerian parentage; like Cathy Freeman, he had overcome discrimination and crossed boundaries in his long career.

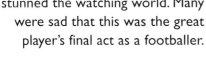

Zidane's attack on Materazzi stunned the watching world. Many were sad that this was the great player's final act as a footballer.

Some media stories claimed that the Italian defender had called Zidane a 'terrorist'. After the game, Zidane claimed that insults about his mother and sister had caused him to react. Materazzi admitted insulting Zidane, but said that his words were trivial.

Reaction to the incident was mixed. French president Jacques Chirac hailed Zidane as a national hero and called him a 'man of heart and conviction'. However, French newspaper Le Figaro called the incident 'unacceptable'. Another paper wondered how the icon Zidane would explain his actions to 'millions of children around the world'.

• Up for discussion •

Despite his red card, Zidane was awarded the Golden Ball as the best player of the 2006 World Cup finals. His sponsors also announced that they would stick with him. Should the media and sponsors support unsportsmanlike behaviour? What sort of message does that send out?

Media overkill

With 24-hour sports channels, specialist newspapers and magazines and millions of sports-mad websites, is there too much sport in the media? And does the media have too big an impact on how sports are played?

Many people, including Sky TV soccer pundit Andy Gray, think so. In 2005, he admitted that he felt there were too many games on TV. With so many broadcast matches, and so many newspaper pages devoted to football coverage, Gray worried that viewers would become bored of the game.

Taking over

Sport reaches a tipping point when marketing considerations become more important than the competition itself. Football was famously manipulated to make it more television-friendly in the USA. The game was divided into quarters, and exciting shoot-outs replaced boring score-draws. Televised wrestling bouts in the USA are the most extreme example of the media's power to turn sport into circus. In the WWE (World Wrestling Entertainment) league, acting skills are just as important as sporting ability.

Outrageous moves and crazy stunts keep millions of WWE viewers worldwide entertained.

The first season of the Twenty20 cricket competition, the Indian Premier League (IPL), took place in 2008. The IPL so far looks set to be a big commercial success, generating millions of pounds in broadcasting deals alone. But not everyone has been thrilled by the tournament. Twenty20 is a new cricket format. It is fast-paced, exciting and more suited to television viewing than traditional test match cricket. But some say that the new format threatens the traditional skills of the game.

The organisers of the IPL have also managed to upset various cricket boards around the world. The main argument is that players should always be available to play for their country, and the IPL season takes place in the middle of a number of international tours.

The IPL has also angered sections of the media. To protect its image, strict guidelines on IPL media coverage were introduced. Press agencies were forced to upload all photos taken at matches onto an official IPL website. After the threat of a media boycott of matches, the IPL relaxed some restrictions. Several major photo agencies, including Reuters and AFP, still refuse to cover the IPL, however.

India captain Mahendra Singh Dhoni's playing talent and good looks have combined to make him the public face of the IPL.

• *Up for discussion* •

The IPL has been criticised for introducing cricket cheerleaders. This marketing ploy is popular with many spectators. But some people say it goes against the traditional spirit of the game. Others argue it might upset some Indian sensibilities. What do you think?

Sporting scandals

One of the great benefits of intense media coverage of sports is that it both celebrates sporting feats accomplished by clean athletes, and exposes the cheats.

The media has had a crucial part to play in exposing some of the greatest sporting scandals. Stars who take drugs or who accept bribes to fix the results of matches not only risk the attention of sporting authorities, but also of investigative journalists.

Scoop!

One of the most infamous episodes in US sports history is the 'Black Sox' Scandal of 1919. Hugh Fullerton was a reporter for the *Chicago Herald and Examiner*. He was due to cover the baseball World Series between the Chicago White Sox and Cincinnati Reds. Fullerton received a tip from professional gamblers that the Cincinnati team was a 'safe bet' to win.

As Fullerton watched the series, the reporter counted the number of suspicious plays. He then wrote a series of articles, headlined 'Is Big League Baseball Being Run for Gamblers, with Ballplayers in the Deal?' This forced the baseball establishment to investigate

THE CHANGING WORLD

[Copyright: 1920: By The Chicago Tribune.]

"THE BEAUTY ABOUT BASE BALL IS THAT IT'S ALWAYS BEEN KEPT STRAIGHT AND CLEAN"

POLITICS   HIGH FINANCE

PUGILISM   HORSE RACING   BASE BALL

Our national sport as it has been regarded.   *It now joins the "Black Eye club."*

A newspaper cartoon pokes fun at baseball's Black Sox scandal.

the charges, and it was discovered that players had been accepting bribes to fix the results of games to suit gamblers. One year later, eight White Sox ballplayers were banned from the game for life for 'throwing' or fixing games.

Media pressure

The media is quick to seize on any story of wrong-doing. Drug cheats at major sporting events are front-page news. Athletics and cycling are two sports that have had huge problems with athletes who use performance-enhancing drugs in recent years. The sporting authorities do their best to police this with drug-testing programs. But the media also plays its part in outing the cheats, and discouraging those who might have been tempted. Athletes who are under suspicion will be under a great deal of scrutiny at events like the Olympic Games.

• Up for discussion •

The rewards for sporting success are so great that perhaps today's modern stars dare not fail. How can the media be seen to encourage this 'win-at-all-costs' attitude?

Case study: Fall from grace

One of the most successful US athletes of recent times was Marion Jones. She won five medals at the 2000 Summer Olympics in Sydney, Australia. But she has since been stripped of every medal. Jones had long been suspected of taking steroids. Although this is a common allegation surrounding track and field athletes, Jones had also worked with a number of controversial coaches. But she always denied the rumours.

The media finally caught up with Jones. The founder of a company that produces performance-enhancing drugs appeared in an interview on the US TV show 20/20. He admitted that he had personally given Jones five different illegal drugs.

A tearful Marion Jones faces the media after admitting taking banned steroids.

Pushing the
boundaries

Rivalry between nations or regions adds spice to a sporting event. The media can play its part in whipping up a frenzy of national pride during international competitions. Meanwhile, some stars have used the sports field to express pride in their race, political beliefs or lifestyle.

Bad sportsmanship

Golf's Ryder Cup takes place every two years between two teams of players from Europe and the USA. It is a fiercely contested competition and players are urged on by supporters on both sides, but a 'gentleman's' code of conduct is usually observed.

At the 1999 Ryder Cup however, the US team staged a stirring comeback to all but win the competition and their fans celebrated wildly, storming the green before the European player had even taken his last shot. The European media was disgusted by the reaction of the US players and, in particular, the supporters whom they accused of breaking golf's code of conduct, and 'winning a Cup, but losing all dignity'.

US golfer Tiger Woods celebrates a successful shot on the tenth hole at the 1999 Ryder Cup with players and fans.

Case study: Making a stand

Zimbabwe cricketers Henry Olonga and Andy Flower attracted worldwide media attention in 2003. The players took to the field in a Cricket World Cup match wearing black armbands. These were a symbol of protest against the policies of Zimbabwe's government, led by Robert Mugabe.

The players issued the following press statement : 'It is impossible to ignore what is happening in Zimbabwe. Although we are just professional cricketers, we do have a conscience and feelings. We believe that if we remain silent that will be taken as a sign that either we do not care or we [support] what is happening in Zimbabwe. We believe that it is important to stand up for what is right.'

Olonga and Flower are proud Zimbabweans. They used the power of the media to draw attention to the tragic events in their country. Sadly, their brave protest led to pressure from Zimbabwe's government on the players, who were forced to retire from international cricket.

Henry Olonga fled Zimbabwe in 2003 and now lives in England, where he works as a commentator and singer.

• Up for discussion •

'Sport and politics don't mix'.
Do you agree with this statement?
If so, why?

The race game

The media has the power to decide which athletes receive the most attention. But it celebrates the achievements of all participants, whatever their ethnic background. This is because of the brave efforts of athletes who have broken through racial barriers and changed the way that sport is played.

Protest

Until the 1960s, in parts of the USA, black people were kept apart from white people in many aspects of life, including sport. At the 1968 Olympic Games, US athletes Tommy Smith and John Carlos famously raised their fists during the men's 200 metre medal ceremony. Their actions were a protest against discrimination against black people in the USA. They realised that they could use the power of the media in sport to take a stand against racism in all American life.

Smith and Carlos' powerful gesture became front-page news around the world.

• Up for discussion •

Smith and Carlos were booed by the crowd and widely criticised in the media for their protest in 1968. Why is their silent protest now celebrated?

An equal shot

Discrimination on the grounds of race is no longer acceptable in sport and media coverage. In 2006, Australian cricket commentator Dean Jones was sacked after referring to Muslim South African player Hashim Amla as a terrorist. In the UK, football pundit Ron Atkinson was dismissed after using a racist term to describe black player Marcel Desailly when he thought he was off-air.

Kick It Out is English football's equality and inclusion campaign. It uses the appeal of the game, as well as the media exposure of football, to challenge discrimination and deliver positive messages of race equality within football. England football captain John Terry says: 'Everyone should be aware of the need to kick racism out of society and football.'

Case study: The Anti-Apartheid Movement

Apartheid was a set of segregation laws passed in 1948 in South Africa. These laws forbade, among many other things, all multiracial sport. Touring sporting teams were forced to exclude non-white players.

Sport in South Africa is traditionally a central and highly competitive part of the white community. The Anti-Apartheid Movement therefore targeted it as an area to spearhead change. They used the power of the media to gain coverage of a campaign of disruption. In 1969, the South African rugby team's tour of the UK was dogged by anti-Apartheid campaigners, who invaded the pitch before and during games.

Rugby and cricket authorities around the world were soon forced to ban their teams and players from playing against South Africa. Further pressure from the Anti-Apartheid Movement eventually led to a sporting boycott of South Africa, which lasted until the early 1990s when Apartheid was abolished.

Kick It Out's website urges people who have witnessed racism at a football match to report it and 'out' the racists.

Fighting discrimination

In recent years, another black athlete has used US professional sport and the media attention it attracts to focus on discrimination against individuals because of their sexuality.

Case study: Crossing the line

John Amaechi has always been an outsider. He is black and is one of the few British basketball players to have made it in the NBA. He is also intelligent and well-spoken. Amaechi is not a typical NBA player. Nevertheless, he enjoyed a successful playing career.

In 2007, Amaechi distanced himself even further from the media image of the 'typical' NBA star by announcing that he was gay on ESPN's Outside the Lines TV programme. According to reports, Amaechi's announcement 'sent shockwaves throughout the sporting world'. He was the first NBA basketball player to come out, and one of only a handful of US sports stars to admit that they were gay.

Amaechi's announcement was a huge story in the media. But Amaechi forced the NBA to publicly state its tolerance. 'We have a very diverse league. The question at the NBA is always, "Have you got game?" That's it, end of inquiry,' said NBA Commissioner David Stern.

Since retiring from the NBA, Amaechi has used his experience to build a successful media career. He has presented TV coverage of NBA basketball and manages a company of motivational speakers.

John Amaechi speaks at the GLAAD (Gay & Lesbian Alliance Against Defamation) media awards in 2007.

Young talent

British footballer Justin Fashanu was not as fortunate as John Amaechi. Fashanu was a very gifted young player who first hit the newspaper headlines in 1981 when he became the first black British player to command a £1 million transfer fee. But Fashanu's football career started to fade at about the same time as rumours and stories about his personal life began to circulate in the media.

Coming out

In 1990, Fashanu became the first professional footballer in Britain to come out. He agreed to an exclusive interview with *The Sun* newspaper, which ran a '£1m Football Star: I AM GAY' headline and gave details about some of the men that Fashanu had had relations with.

Fashanu was interviewed by the *Gay Times* in 1991. He admitted that he hadn't been prepared for the backlash that had followed his announcement, and believed that his football career had suffered 'heavy damage' as a result of it. The anti-gay crowd abuse that Fashanu suffered revealed the deep-seated prejudice against homosexuals in the English game, which Fashanu blamed for the end of his footballing career. In a tragic conclusion, he eventually committed suicide in 1998.

Footballer Justin Fashanu in 1990, shortly before he officially came out.

• Up for discussion •

Why do you think many gay sportsmen and women feel the need to hide their sexuality from the media's glare?

John Amaechi's former Orlando Magic teammate Grant Hill said, 'The fact that John has done this, maybe it will give others the comfort or confidence to come out as well.' Do you think he was right?

Tackling inequality

The success and bravery of some athletes has broken down barriers in race and sexuality in sport and society. The same is true for athletes with disabilities. However, some see continuing inequalities in media coverage of women's sport.

The Paralympics

The Paralympics – the games contested by disabled athletes – barely received any media attention up until the 1990s. But by 2008, the Paralympics were being shown on television in many countries. The media now gives equal recognition to the achievements of athletes with disabilities. Some disabled athletes, such as South African Oscar Pistorius (below) and British wheelchair athlete Dame Tanni Grey Thompson, have become celebrated media figures in their own right.

Sideshow

Discrimination in the media approach to female sports continues, however. Coverage lags way behind that of men's events and as much interest is shown in competitors' looks as in how they perform. In 2008, the UK's Women's Sport and Fitness Foundation looked at national daily newspapers and found that 'just 2% of articles and 1% of images in the sports pages were devoted to female athletes and women's sports'. A sample study

Double amputee Oscar Pistorius, who runs on artificial limbs, was a popular media figure at the 2008 Paralympics.

The Olympic Games is one of the few sporting occasions in which male and female athletes receive equal coverage, and women's athletic ability, rather than their looks, remains the focus. 'What's great with the Olympics is the immediacy of it all – you see the women competing, and then they're on the rostrum straight away, looking incredibly natural,' says one commentator.

The strong performances by female athletes at the 2008 Olympic Games did a lot to fight back against the media's usual presentation. Britain's rain-soaked gold medal cyclist Nicole Cooke was one of the Games' stars. One sports writer said: 'Here was a woman being celebrated for her power rather than her femininity. This wasn't about how Nicole Cooke looked, or what her success could sell, or who she might or might not be sponsored by. This was about Nicole Cooke and her will to win.'

Welsh cyclist Nicole Cooke takes gold for Team Great Britain in the 2008 Olympic Road Race.

also revealed that out of a total of 72 hours of Sky TV sports programming, just three hours were given over to women's events.

At worst, attitudes to women's sport can be sexist. FIFA president Sepp Blatter has urged women footballers to wear skimpier kits to increase the popularity of the women's game. At best, media coverage of women's sport can seem like a sideshow to the men's events, with the focus on the fashions and looks of competitors.

• *Up for discussion* •

The WSFF study showed that just 1.4% of sports photography featured women. Although research only looked at the sports pages, there were more images of models and footballers' girlfriends. Why is the public more interested in these figures than in real female competitors?

Future stories

In newspapers, television and on the Internet, sporting events are often over-hyped, in some cases making or breaking stars overnight. What is our fascination with sport?

Sports sells

For many, sport is much more than just entertainment. It can exert a powerful grip over people's emotions, inspiring loyalty, pride, patriotism and even anger. The media's role in sport is so significant because it reflects and reports these emotions. The passion of sports fans, wherever they are in the world and whatever sport they follow, ensures that the media will always have an audience and thus the media's huge impact on sport is set to continue.

Celebrating the success stories

Global media coverage and the rise of marketing, sponsorship and endorsements has meant that success in many professional sports is now measured in terms of money. But elevating sports events to much more than a game puts incredible pressure on athletes to succeed. And it can come at the expense of sportsmanship and fair play.

However, the media also celebrates 'clean' winners and challenges cheating, sending out a strong moral message.

Media coverage has also allowed athletes from all walks of life to demonstrate pride in their performance to the rest of the world – sometimes overcoming great personal and social barriers to do so. Perhaps most importantly, positive media coverage can help to inspire the young athletes of tomorrow to follow their heroes and take part in sports themselves.

• Up for discussion •

Why do you think people are so interested in sport?

Do you follow any sports yourself? How do you find out about them?

Case study: Young stars

British diver Tom Daley is 14 years old. He was one of the youngest competitors at the 2008 Olympic Games, and also had a genuine shot at glory. His ability excited the media around the world. In the run-up to the Games, spectator seats at Daley's training pool were full of journalists, and camera crews milled around at the bottom of the diving platforms.

Tom is used to being the focus of media attention. He has also used the power of the new media to great effect. Every one of his dives is filmed and posted on YouTube and fans can leave comments and messages of encouragement on his website.

17-year-old US gymnast Shawn Johnson also took part in the Beijing 2008 Olympic Games, winning a gold medal in the balance beam and silver in the all-round competition. It was the highest point to date in a glittering athletic career, which has been followed with keen media interest.

Shawn has already appeared on numerous TV shows including the famous Today Show, and has taken part in the US TV show Dancing with the Stars. Shawn has also featured in magazines including Vanity Fair and Teen Vogue. She uses the Internet to keep in touch with her funs via her website and blog.

Glossary

Ambassador An official representative of an organisation or movement.

Apartheid A political system in South Africa from 1948 to the early 1990s that separated the different races living there and gave privileges to white people.

Aryan In Nazi ideology, a white, non-Jewish person, thought to be racially superior.

Boycott Refusal to deal with a country, organisation or company, as a protest against it or as an attempt to force it to change its ways.

Brand name A trade name for a product or service produced by a particular company.

Cold War The hostile yet nonviolent relations between the former USSR and the USA, and their respective allies, from 1946 to 1989.

Come out To declare openly that one is gay or lesbian.

Commercial Relating to the buying and selling of goods or services.

Discrimination Unfair treatment of one person or group, usually because of prejudice about race, sexuality, age, religion or gender.

Endorsement Giving public approval of a product for advertising purposes.

Fair play Playing by the rules.

Hype Overkill; greatly exaggerated publicity intended to excite public interest in a young sports star.

Icon A person who is widely admired.

Merchandise Goods for sale.

Motivational speaker An individual who publicly addresses an audience to inspire enthusiasm, interest or commitment.

Performance-enhancing drugs Banned substances, such as steroids, that improve an athlete's ability to train or their performance.

Pole position In motor racing, the best starting position.

Press statement An official account of a news story that is prepared and issued to newspapers and other news media for them to make known to the public.

Professionalism Competing in sport for financial gain rather than as an amateur.

Publicity Information about a person or event that is circulated in the media to attract public interest.

Propaganda Information put out by an organisation or government to promote an idea or cause.

Pundit A personality who expresses opinions on a subject, for example football.

Racism Prejudice against people who belong to other races.

Rights In media, rights are legal agreements that allow a media outlet to broadcast a game or show.

Role model A worthy person who sets a good example for other people to follow.

Saturate To fill something so completely that nothing else can be added to it.

Sponsorship When a person or organisation provides money to help fund an event or group.

Sportsmanship Fair play, respect for other competitors and graciousness in losing.

Stock market An organised market where brokers meet to buy and sell stocks and shares.

Terrorist A person who uses violent methods, such as bombing, kidnapping and assassination, to intimidate others, often for political purposes.

Throw Intentionally lose a game.

Tipping point A defining moment in a series of events.

Tolerance The acceptance of different views of other people, for example in religious or political matters.

Tycoon An individual with great wealth and power, especially in business.

UN The United Nations; an organisation of nations that was formed in 1945 to promote peace, security and international cooperation.

UNICEF A United Nations agency that works for the protection of children around the world.

Further information

Books

British Issues: Sporting Success by Jim Kerr (Franklin Watts, 2008)

Issues in Sport Series Editor Craig Donnellan (Independence, 2003)

Man in the Middle by John Amaechi (ESPN Books, 2007)

Sport in Society by Kirk Bizley (Heinemann, 1997)

Websites

www.community.t20.com
The official site of the Indian Premier League cricket competition. It features news, scorecards, videos and photos.

www.formula1.com
The official Formula One website. It includes news, photos and interviews with the drivers.

www.kickitout.org
The official site of the Let's Kick Racism Out of Football campaign.

www.london2012.com/en
The official website of the 2012 London Olympic Games.

www.olympic.org/uk/index_uk.asp
The official site of the International Olympic Committee (IOC) provides a variety of information on host cities, events, IOC policies and international sports federations.

www.nba.com
The official site of the US National Basketball Association (NBA) includes news, features, multimedia, player profiles, schedules and statistics.

www.paralympic.org
The official website of the International Paralympic Committee.

www.rydercup.com
The official website of the Ryder Cup competition.

www.wimbledon.org
The official website of the Wimbledon Lawn Tennis Championships.

Note to parents and teachers: Every effort has been made by the Publishers to ensure that these websites are suitable for children, that they are of the highest educational value, and that they contain no inappropriate or offensive material. However, because of the nature of the Internet, it is impossible to guarantee that the contents of these sites will not be altered. We strongly advise that Internet access is supervised by a responsible adult.

Index

Numbers in bold refer to captions to illustrations.

These are the list of contents for each title in *Media Power*.